Comptroller of the Currency
Administrator of National Banks

US Department of the Treasury

2011 **Survey of Credit Underwriting Practices**

Contents

Survey of Credit Underwriting Practices
2011

Introduction

The Office of the Comptroller of the Currency (OCC) conducted its 17th annual underwriting survey to identify trends in lending standards and credit risk for the most common types of commercial and retail credit offered by national banks. The survey covers the 12-month period ending February 28, 2011.

The 2011 survey includes examiner assessments of credit underwriting standards at 54 of the largest national banks with assets of $3 billion or more. Examiners reported on loan products greater than 2 percent of the company's committed loan portfolio or more than $10 billion in committed exposure. The OCC recognizes that banks may offer many other products not meeting these thresholds; however, because of the size of the product portfolios, examiners did not gather information on them for the purposes of this report. The survey covers loans totaling $4.2 trillion as of December 31, 2010, which represents approximately 94 percent of total loans in the national banking system at that time. Large banks discussed in this report are the 14 largest banks by asset size supervised by the OCC's Large Bank Supervision Department; the other 40 banks are supervised by the OCC's Midsize and Community Bank Supervision Department.

OCC examiners assigned to each bank assessed overall credit trends for 20 commercial and retail credit products. For the purposes of this survey, commercial credit includes the following 13 categories:

- agricultural
- asset-based lending
- commercial construction
- residential construction
- other commercial real estate
- commercial leasing
- international
- large corporate
- leveraged
- middle market
- small business
- hedge funds (direct lending exposure)
- hedge funds (counterparty credit exposure)

Retail credit includes the following seven categories:

- affordable housing
- credit cards
- indirect consumer paper
- conventional home equity
- high loan-to-value (HLTV) home equity
- other direct consumer
- residential first mortgages

Underwriting standards, as used in this report, refers to the terms and conditions under which banks extend or renew credit, such as financial and collateral requirements, repayment programs, maturities, pricing, and covenants. Conclusions about "easing" or "tightening" represent OCC examiners' observations during the 12-month survey period ending February 28, 2011. A conclusion that the underwriting standards for a particular loan category eased or tightened does not necessarily indicate an adjustment in all the standards for that particular category. Rather, the conclusion indicates that the adjustments that did occur had the net effect of easing or tightening the aggregate conditions under which banks extended credit.

Part I of this report summarizes the overall findings of the survey. Part II shows the survey findings in data graphs. Part III presents the raw data used to develop the survey's principal findings and to create the data graphs. (Note: Some percentages in tables and figures do not add to 100 because of rounding.)

Part I: Overall Results

Primary Findings

- The results of this year's survey show some signs of easing, especially in commercial products. Underwriting standards remain in transition as banks continue to react to economic conditions and changing risk in their portfolios. In certain products, banks are once again easing standards in response to competition, an improvement in credit market liquidity, and a desire for more market share. Approximately one third of responses, however, show banks continue to tighten standards for products with high losses. Generally, large banks have the highest share of easing credit underwriting.

- Loan portfolios that experience the most easing in underwriting include indirect consumer, international, large corporate, asset-based lending, and leveraged loans. Loan portfolios that experience the most tightening in underwriting during the 2011 survey period include credit card, home equity, commercial and residential construction, and residential real estate loans.

- As in the past, the health of the economy is a major factor influencing the tightening of credit standards. Expectations regarding the future health of the economy, however, differ by bank and loan product as examiners report that the economic outlook is one of the main reasons given for tightening or easing underwriting standards. Other factors influencing tighter underwriting standards are a change in risk appetite and product performance. Additional factors contributing to easing standards are changes in the competitive environment, market liquidity, and market penetration strategies.

- Since the 2010 survey, the change in the level of credit risk is mixed in both commercial and retail portfolios. Approximately one-third of the loan products have increased credit risk, one-third have decreased credit risk, and one-third have the same level of credit risk when compared with 12 months ago. Over the next 12 months, examiners believe that credit risk will likely increase for 36 percent of the loan products, decrease for 22 percent, and remain unchanged for 42 percent.

- Similar to the results of the 2010 survey, this year's survey indicates that the majority of banks generally apply the same underwriting standards to loans underwritten with the intent to hold as to those underwritten with the intent to sell.

Commentary on Credit Risk

The greatest credit risk in banks is the ongoing impact of real estate values due to the significant volume of commercial real estate, residential real estate, and home equity loans in national banks' portfolios. Banks with significant credit card portfolios have experienced significant credit risk due to the impact of the weak economy and high unemployment rate.

Some banks continue to have higher credit risk due to the recent financial market downturn, and those banks continue to tighten underwriting standards in response. Many banks continue to struggle with high levels of classified credits and declining collateral values. These factors, along with uncertainty about the economic outlook, contributed to the continued tightening or unchanged underwriting standards in many banks. Other banks are beginning to ease underwriting standards in some products to meet loan demand and improve earnings. In large banks, leveraged lending is starting to show significant easing from the relatively tighter standards present during the financial crisis. This change is a result of increasing competition, market liquidity, and desire to improve margins.

As banks begin to ease underwriting standards to meet loan demand and improve earnings, the OCC cautions banks on the need to maintain prudent underwriting standards. The OCC expects national banks to underwrite loans based on sound underwriting standards, regardless of their intent to hold or sell the loan, and to apply the same general standards for both types of lending.

Examiners report tightening of overall commercial underwriting standards in 32 percent of the banks and of overall retail underwriting standards in 30 percent of the banks. Easing of overall commercial underwriting standards is reported in 20 percent of the banks and easing of overall retail underwriting standards in 7 percent of the banks. Loan products that experienced the most tightening are credit card, home equity, commercial and residential construction, and residential real estate loans. Loan products that experienced the most easing are indirect consumer, international, large corporate, asset-based lending, and leveraged loans.

The surveyed banks use pricing as their primary method to ease underwriting standards for commercial products. Pricing and score card cutoffs are used to ease underwriting standards for retail products. In banks where standards are being tightened, collateral requirements and loan covenants (except leverage) are most frequently used to tighten commercial standards, while score cards, debt service requirements, and collateral requirements are used to tighten retail standards. In most products, the survey shows fewer approved exceptions to policy.

The survey shows that examiners' expectations for the overall level of credit risk is unchanged or improving over the next 12 months in more than 60 percent of the responses. This is a significant improvement from last year's survey. In the 2010 survey, more than 60 percent of the responses showed an expectation for an increasing level of risk over the next 12 months. In instances where increasing risk for products is still expected, the primary reasons listed are the state of the economy, high levels of problem loans, and continued downward pressure on real estate values.

Commercial Underwriting Standards

The number of banks where examiners report a net easing in commercial credit standards increased significantly. As presented in table 1, the 2011 survey results show that 20 percent of the surveyed banks eased commercial underwriting standards. This is a clear shift in standards after the last three years, when the majority of banks were tightening standards. The majority of reported easing is in large banks.

Table 1: Commercial Products

	2005	2006	2007	2008	2009	2010	2011
Eased	34%	31%	26%	6%	0%	2%	20%
Unchanged	54%	63%	58%	42%	14%	33%	48%
Tightened	12%	6%	16%	52%	86%	65%	32%

Note: For additional information, see figure 1 on page 15.

The survey shows mixed economic expectations for the future. In some cases, examiners report that bankers cited an improving economic outlook as a reason for easing underwriting standards, while other bankers cited an uncertain economic outlook as a reason for tightening standards. In addition to the economic outlook, examiners report a changed risk appetite and product performance as the primary reasons for tightened standards. On the other hand, they report a changed competitive environment and market liquidity as reasons for easing standards. The return of liquidity in secondary markets is a key contributor to easing standards in the leveraged finance syndicated loan markets and certain commercial real estate (CRE) products.

In recent years, pricing and loan fees—or the compensation for assuming credit risk—were the primary underwriting method that banks used to manage the credit risk in their loan portfolios through tightened underwriting standards. Now, some banks are starting to lower loan fees and rates, indicating that competition is once again driving an easing in pricing. Other areas that warrant monitoring where easing is noted include longer loan maturities, higher leverage, and fewer loan covenants. As previously noted, the OCC expects banks to maintain prudent underwriting standards as the economy recovers and competition increases.

Examiners do not express concern with adherence to underwriting standards, citing good or acceptable adherence to underwriting standards with exceptions well supported for most products. The level of approved exceptions is decreasing in 29 percent of commercial products, while another 53 percent indicated no change in the volume of approved exceptions. Exception tracking is in place for 92 percent of the loan products.

Selected Product Trends

Underwriting standards tightened for some commercial loan products and eased for others. The most prevalent tightening occurs in CRE loans, leasing, and small business loans. The most prevalent easing is in international, large corporate, asset-based lending, and leveraged loans. Large banks typically offer the products with the most easing.

The level and direction of credit risk moved from primarily increasing last year to more of a mix of increasing, unchanged, and decreasing. This is consistent with broad trends in commercial credit quality, which generally show stabilization or improvement even though credit quality indicators remain at elevated levels. Small business and middle market loans still had sizable increasing levels of credit risk responses, while leasing and asset-based loans had significant net decreasing levels of risk responses.

Commercial Real Estate

CRE products include residential construction, commercial construction, and other CRE loans. Almost all of the surveyed banks offered at least one of these CRE products. CRE remains a primary concern of examiners, given the current economic environment and some banks' significant concentrations relative to their capital. While the majority of banks' underwriting standards remain unchanged for CRE, net tightening, which measures the difference between the percentage of banks tightening and the percentage of those easing, is greatest in residential construction, followed by commercial construction, and other commercial real estate. Examiners cite the distressed real estate market, poor product performance, and reduced risk appetite as the main reasons for banks' net tightening.

Examiners' responses on the level and direction of credit risk in CRE continue to show improvement. All products still show some level of increasing risk but the majority of responses are for declining or unchanged risk. "Other CRE" is the only product where the number of increasing risk responses is higher for the future 12-month period. Driving examiners' assessment of increased credit risk are external conditions, downward trends in collateral values, weakening debt service capacity, and current and expected levels of problem loans. The banks with an assessment of decreasing credit risk are in areas where the economy and property values have begun to stabilize, or the bank has been able to work through its weaker credits, leaving a stronger portfolio.

The next three tables provide the breakdown by each real estate type.

Of the 54 banks in the survey, 19 (or 35 percent) offer residential construction loan products. These products' recent performance has been poor, and many banks have either exited the product or significantly curtailed new originations. Weak initial underwriting, compounded by weak economic conditions, has resulted in high levels of problem loans and losses. Table 2 shows that 63 percent of banks offering the product in 2011 maintained similar underwriting standards for residential construction, 37 percent continued to tighten underwriting standards, while none reported easing standards.

Table 2: Residential Construction

	2005	2006	2007	2008	2009	2010	2011
Eased	21%	25%	17%	2%	0%	0%	0%
Unchanged	72%	64%	50%	36%	8%	36%	63%
Tightened	7%	11%	33%	62%	92%	64%	37%

Note: For additional information, see tables on page 29.

Thirty-three banks (or 61 percent) offer commercial construction loans. The economic environment has adversely affected collateral values, which have not stabilized in many areas. Table 3 shows that the majority of underwriting standards for commercial construction remain unchanged, while 36 percent of banks offering commercial construction tightened underwriting standards and only 3 percent reported easing standards.

Table 3: Commercial Construction

	2005	2006	2007	2008	2009	2010	2011
Eased	29%	32%	28%	8%	0%	3%	3%
Unchanged	63%	56%	59%	43%	20%	25%	61%
Tightened	8%	12%	13%	49%	80%	72%	36%

Note: For additional information, see tables on page 28.

Nearly all banks (52 of 54) offered a variety of CRE loans for purposes other than residential or commercial construction. For purposes of this survey, the OCC broadly groups these loans under the "Other CRE" category. As with commercial residential and commercial construction loans, the survey shows that the economic environment, particularly depressed collateral values, is affecting risk in this loan category. Table 4 shows that 33 percent of the banks offering "Other CRE" tightened underwriting standards for the product while 10 percent eased standards.

Table 4: Other CRE

	2005	2006	2007	2008	2009	2010	2011
Eased	24%	32%	20%	2%	2%	2%	10%
Unchanged	65%	60%	73%	73%	22%	38%	58%
Tightened	11%	8%	7%	25%	76%	60%	33%

Note: For additional information, see tables on page 30.

Leveraged Loans

While only 16 (or 30 percent) of the banks meet the threshold for reporting on this product, the size of the portfolio is significant. Table 5 shows that 37 percent of banks offering leveraged loans eased underwriting standards while 19 percent reported tightening standards. When banks were easing standards, increased competition, risk appetite, and market liquidity were the main reasons for easing. Mixed views of economic outlooks contributed to both easing and tightening of standards in different banks. Changes in the banks' risk appetite contributed to tightened standards.

Examiners report that the level of credit risk in leveraged loans increased in six banks and decreased in six banks, while the remaining banks had the same level of credit risk compared with last year's survey. Examiners expect that the credit risk in this product will likely increase at 69 percent of the banks over the next year. This expected increase is due to competition and increasing market liquidity driven by banks' and investors' pursuit of more earning assets, which cause bankers to ease underwriting standards, lower pricing, and require fewer covenants. In the months following this survey, the OCC has noted further easing in underwriting standards for leveraged loans.

Table 5: Leveraged Loans

	2005	2006	2007	2008	2009	2010	2011
Eased	32%	61%	67%	20%	0%	0%	37%
Unchanged	68%	31%	33%	20%	31%	25%	44%
Tightened	0%	8%	0%	60%	69%	75%	19%

Note: For additional information, see tables on page 34.

Small Business Loans

Examiners report that 33 of the 54 surveyed banks offer small business loans. The OCC notes that definitions of small business lending vary among the surveyed banks. Regardless of varying definitions, however, just over half of the banks have underwriting that remains unchanged, while one-third tightened underwriting. The focus of the tightening is on collateral and debt service requirements. Changes in the small business's financial condition, combined with the economic outlook and quality and performance of the portfolio, are the major reasons for tightened credit. Competition and a change in market strategy are the main reasons for those easing credit underwriting standards.

Examiners indicate that small business credit risk increased in 45 percent of the banks offering small business loans since the prior survey and expect the risk will continue to increase over the next year in 36 percent of the banks. Changes in external conditions and portfolio quality are most frequently reported as reasons for the increased level of risk. Table 6 shows that 33 percent of banks offering the product tightened underwriting standards for small business loans, but 12 percent report easing standards. Even with a few banks easing, examiners indicate current underwriting standards at all banks remain either conservative (55 percent) or moderate (45 percent).

Table 6: Small Business Loans

	2005	2006	2007	2008	2009	2010	2011
Eased	13%	19%	11%	11%	0%	0%	12%
Unchanged	81%	76%	76%	72%	36%	34%	55%
Tightened	6%	5%	13%	17%	64%	66%	33%

Note: For additional information, see tables on page 33.

Originate to Hold Versus Originate to Sell

This is the fourth annual survey to assess the differences in underwriting between loans originated to hold in the banks' own loan portfolios and loans originated to sell in the marketplace. The OCC expects national banks to underwrite loans based on sound underwriting standards, regardless of their intent to hold or sell the loan, and to apply the same general standards for both types of lending.

Of all the loan products surveyed, 23 percent were originated both to hold and to sell. In this year's survey, examiners note that 1 of 29 banks offering large corporate loans, 2 of 16 banks offering leveraged loans, and 1 of 9 banks offering international loans had different standards for loans originated to hold than for loans originated to sell. As shown in table 7, there has been significant improvement since 2008 in reducing the differences in underwriting standards. Recent activity shows signs of market resurgence with institutional investors returning to the primary market. The OCC will continue to monitor and assess any differences in underwriting standards for those loans national banks intend to sell and those they intend to hold.

Table 7: Hold Versus Sell Underwriting Standards

	Underwritten differently			
Product	2008	2009	2010	2011
Leveraged loans	67%	38%	12%	13%
International	40%	0%	10%	11%
Large corporate	21%	21%	3%	3%
Asset-based loans	33%	13%	0%	0%
CRE—commercial residential construction	17%	17%	0%	0%
CRE—commercial construction	20%	10%	0%	0%
CRE—other	20%	9%	0%	0%

Retail Underwriting Standards

As noted in table 8, examiners report that most banks either do not change or continue to tighten their overall retail underwriting standards. Retail lending standards were tightened in 30 percent of reporting banks, down from 74 percent in 2010. Examiners note that 62 percent of the banks that tightened underwriting standards during the survey period have conservative underwriting standards while another 31 percent of those banks have moderate underwriting standards. Only one bank that tightened its underwriting standards has standards still considered to be somewhat liberal.

Table 8: Overall Retail Product Underwriting Trends by Banks

	2005	2006	2007	2008	2009	2010	2011
Eased	28%	28%	20%	0%	0%	0%	7%
Unchanged	62%	65%	67%	32%	17%	26%	63%
Tightened	10%	7%	13%	68%	83%	74%	30%

Note: For additional information, see figure 7 on page 20.

Overall, 85 percent of community banks were identified as having conservative underwriting standards, while 57 percent of midsize and 60 percent of large banks were identified as having conservative underwriting standards. In addition, 40 percent of retail products in large banks had standards tightened versus 37 percent in community banks and 23 percent in midsize banks.

Examiners note that banks tightened their underwriting standards for individual products far less this year. Combined, banks tightened standards for 33 percent of individual retail products compared with 58 percent in the 2010 survey. The principal reasons given for tightening specific retail product underwriting standards are changes in economic outlook, risk appetite, and product performance. Underwriting standards were unchanged for 54 percent of retail product offerings, up from 39 percent in the 2010 survey.

The 2011 survey finds that easing of underwriting standards occurred in 13 percent of the individual retail products, up from only 3 percent in the 2010 survey. Changes in market strategy, the competitive environment, and economic outlook are identified as the primary drivers for easing. Despite the easing noted in specific product standards, none of the easing represents a significant change in the underwriting standards for these products.

Examiners report that the credit risk in the majority of retail products was either unchanged or increased modestly. The 2011 responses reflect a shift from the 2010 survey, where examiners indicated that credit risk associated with retail products had mostly increased. In 2010, the level of increased credit risk was most pronounced in credit cards, home equity, residential real estate, and direct consumer lending. The 2011 survey reflects that the quantity of credit risk in credit card portfolios and high loan-to-value home equity loans decreased in 50 percent or more of the banks. While the effects of general economic conditions, legislative and regulatory initiatives, and portfolio performance resulting from prior years' liberal underwriting remain as significant concerns, examiners expect credit risk to remain largely unchanged or even decrease somewhat in most retail products at most banks during the coming year. In almost half the banks, however, examiners indicate that credit risk will increase somewhat in residential real estate and indirect consumer loans.

Examiners do not express concern with adherence to underwriting standards, citing good or acceptable adherence to underwriting standards with exceptions well supported for most products. Exception levels were declining in 30 percent of the banks, while no change in the volume of approved exceptions was noted in another 53 percent. Exception tracking is in place at 93 percent of the responding banks. Instances where exception tracking is lacking are isolated in individual products.

Selected Product Trends

The following sections discuss changes within various product groups.

Residential Real Estate

Examiners reported on residential real estate loans in 48 of the surveyed banks. As shown in table 9, 40 percent of the banks offering residential mortgages continue to tighten underwriting standards. Underwriting standards remain predominately unchanged at 52 percent of these banks after several years of tightening. Four banks eased underwriting standards for residential real estate. Easing is centered in collateral requirements, pricing, score card cutoff, and debt service requirements. Examiners report that underwriting standards remain conservative in response to poor portfolio performance resulting from more liberal underwriting standards in previous years, particularly 2005 through 2007 originations, and continuing economic weakness.

As shown in table 10, examiners note similar results for conventional home equity loans with 36 percent of the 44 banks offering this product tightening their underwriting standards and only 9 percent of those banks easing underwriting standards. Banks continue to exit high loan-to-value home equity lending, with only two of the six banks reporting on this product still offering the product. One of these banks plans to stop offering this product in the next 12 months.

Table 9: Residential Real Estate

	2005	2006	2007	2008	2009	2010	2011
Eased	22%	26%	19%	0%	0%	5%	8%
Unchanged	73%	69%	67%	44%	27%	36%	52%
Tightened	5%	5%	14%	56%	73%	59%	40%

Note: For additional information, see tables on page 44.

Table 10: Home Equity—Conventional

	2005	2006	2007	2008	2009	2010	2011
Eased	27%	34%	19%	2%	0%	5%	9%
Unchanged	62%	64%	65%	46%	22%	35%	55%
Tightened	11%	2%	16%	52%	78%	60%	36%

Note: For additional information, see tables on page 41.

Table 11: Home Equity—High LTV

	2005	2006	2007	2008	2009	2010	2011
Eased	24%	37%	22%	6%	0%	0%	0%
Unchanged	56%	63%	61%	6%	7%	13%	50%
Tightened	20%	0%	17%	89%	93%	87%	50%

Note: For additional information, see tables on page 42.

Credit Cards

As shown in table 12, 44 percent of the 16 banks offering credit cards tightened underwriting standards compared with 81 percent last year. Another 31 percent of the banks left underwriting standards unchanged after significant tightening in prior years. For the first time since the 2008 survey, 25 percent of banks offering credit cards have eased their underwriting standards, primarily in response to changes in economic outlook, the competitive environment, market strategy, and regulatory policy. The principal methods of easing credit card underwriting standards were reducing score card cutoffs and increasing maximum line size.

Examiners report that credit risk in card portfolios increased in only 6 percent of banks compared with 94 percent in the 2010 survey, while credit risk decreased in 69 percent of the banks. Examiners expect that the level of credit risk in this product will remain unchanged in the next year in more than half of the reporting banks and decline in another 25 percent. The rate of increase in credit risk has slowed as the effect of more conservative lending standards has become embedded in the portfolios, the economy improves, and lenders work through existing portfolio problems. Examiners continue to be concerned over the existing level of credit risk in the credit card portfolios but are optimistic as to the direction of risk during the coming year.

Table 12: Credit Cards

	2005	2006	2007	2008	2009	2010	2011
Eased	7%	19%	16%	18%	0%	0%	25%
Unchanged	74%	56%	79%	47%	32%	19%	31%
Tightened	19%	25%	5%	35%	68%	81%	44%

Note: For additional information, see tables on page 39.

Consumer Lending (Direct and Indirect)

Consumer lending often encompasses a variety of products, and banks may have taken different actions with regard to underwriting standards or plans for each product grouped in this section. Further, examiners' conclusions about credit risk or the direction of credit risk may not be the same for all products grouped in this section. When differences exist, the response generally relates to the most significant product, by dollar volume.

In this survey, examiners report on indirect consumer lending in 19 banks and direct consumer lending in 20 banks. Examiners report that 37 percent of indirect lenders and 10 percent of direct lenders eased their underwriting standards. These results represent a notable shift from the 2010 survey, which showed that 60 percent of indirect lenders and one-third of direct lenders tightened underwriting standards. Examiners state that underwriting standards eased owing to changes in market strategy, risk appetite, and improved product performance. The underwriting standards that have changed for these products are primarily pricing and loan fees, score card cutoffs, and collateral requirements.

Ten percent of the banks reporting on indirect consumer lending or direct consumer lending are no longer offering the product. However, four direct and four indirect lenders increased their dollar exposures by more than 10 percent since the last survey, and the same number of banks plan to increase their exposure over the coming year, suggesting a mixed outlook for these products.

Originate to Hold Versus Originate to Sell

Of all retail products, 99 percent are originated to hold while 30 percent are originated for sale. The 2011 survey reports that residential real estate loans are originated for sale by 83 percent of the surveyed banks and affordable housing loans are originated for sale by 25 percent. Approximately 16 percent of the retail products have different underwriting standards for loans originated to sell. Loan pricing, maximum loan amounts, and collateral requirements are the underwriting criteria that most often distinguished loans held in portfolio from those originated for sale. The OCC will continue to monitor and assess any differences in underwriting standards for those loans national banks intend to sell and those they intend to hold.

Part II: Data Graphs

Note: Some percentages used to create the data graphs do not add to 100 because of rounding.

Figure 1: Overall Credit Underwriting Trends—Commercial (Percentage of Responses)

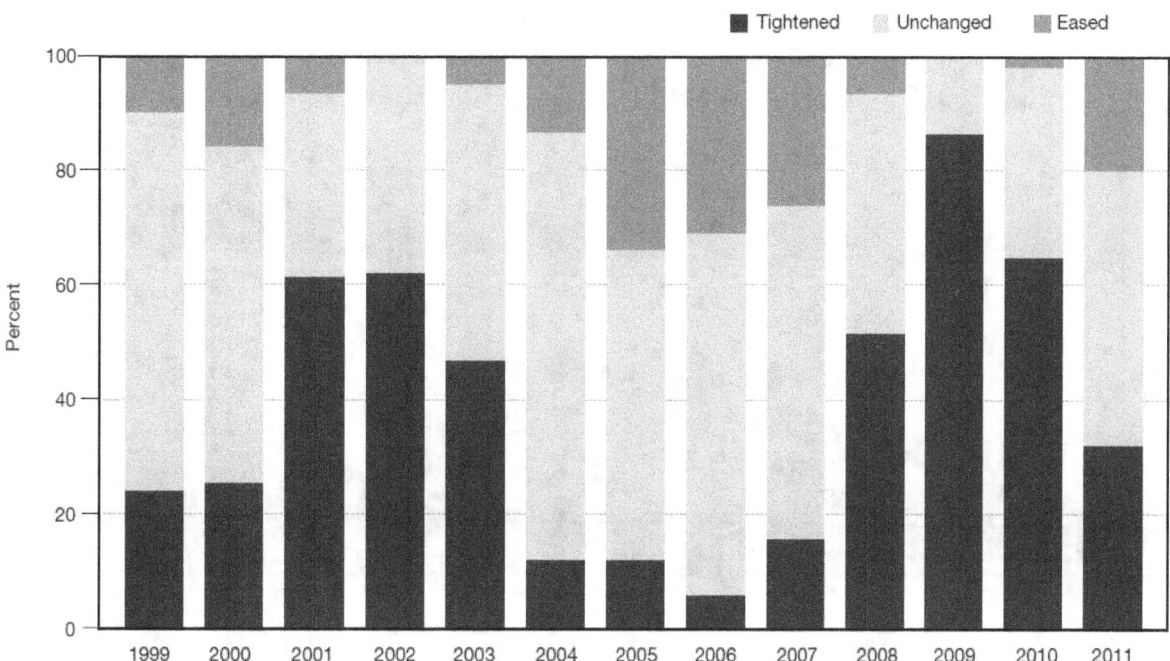

Figure 2: Commercial Underwriting Trends, by Product Type (Percentage of Responses)

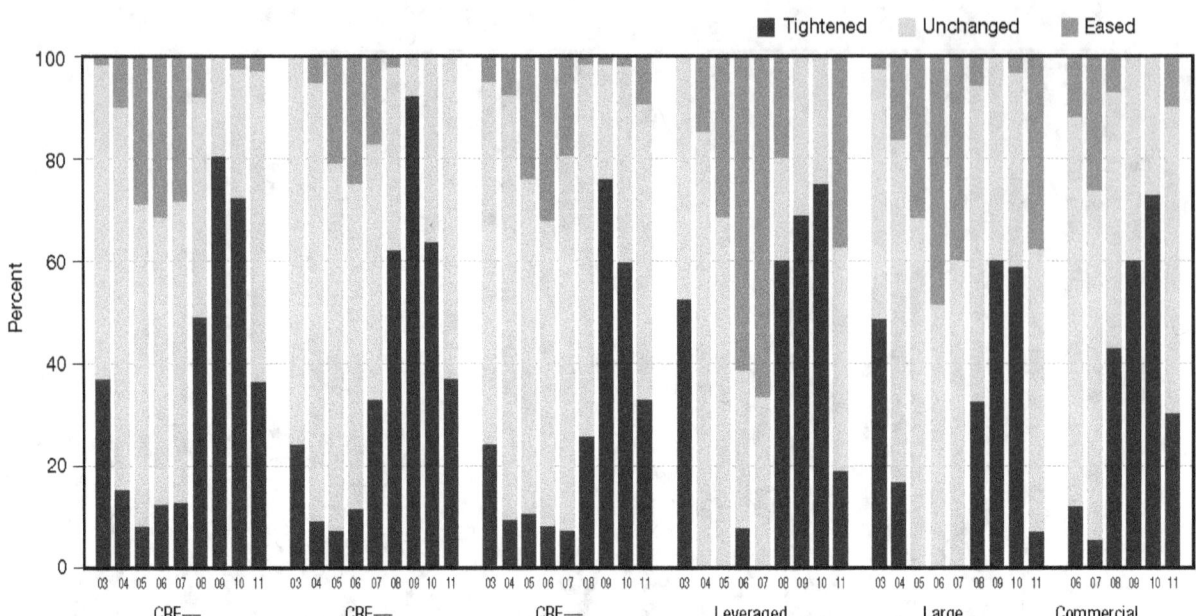

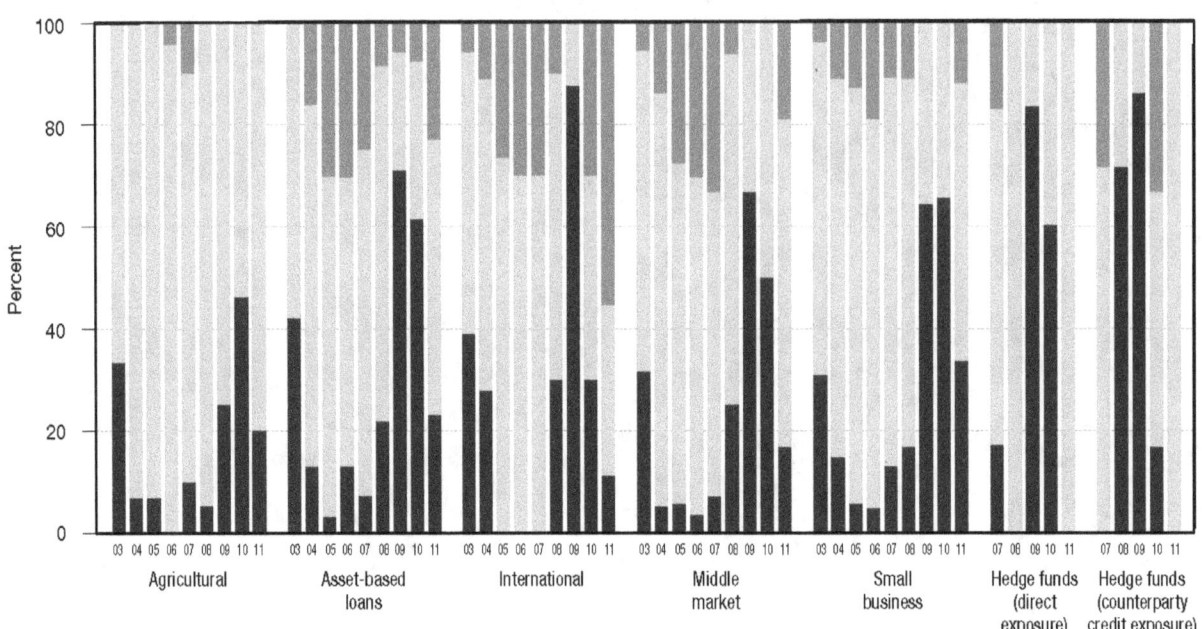

Figure 3: Reasons for Changing Commercial Underwriting Standards (Percentage of Responses)

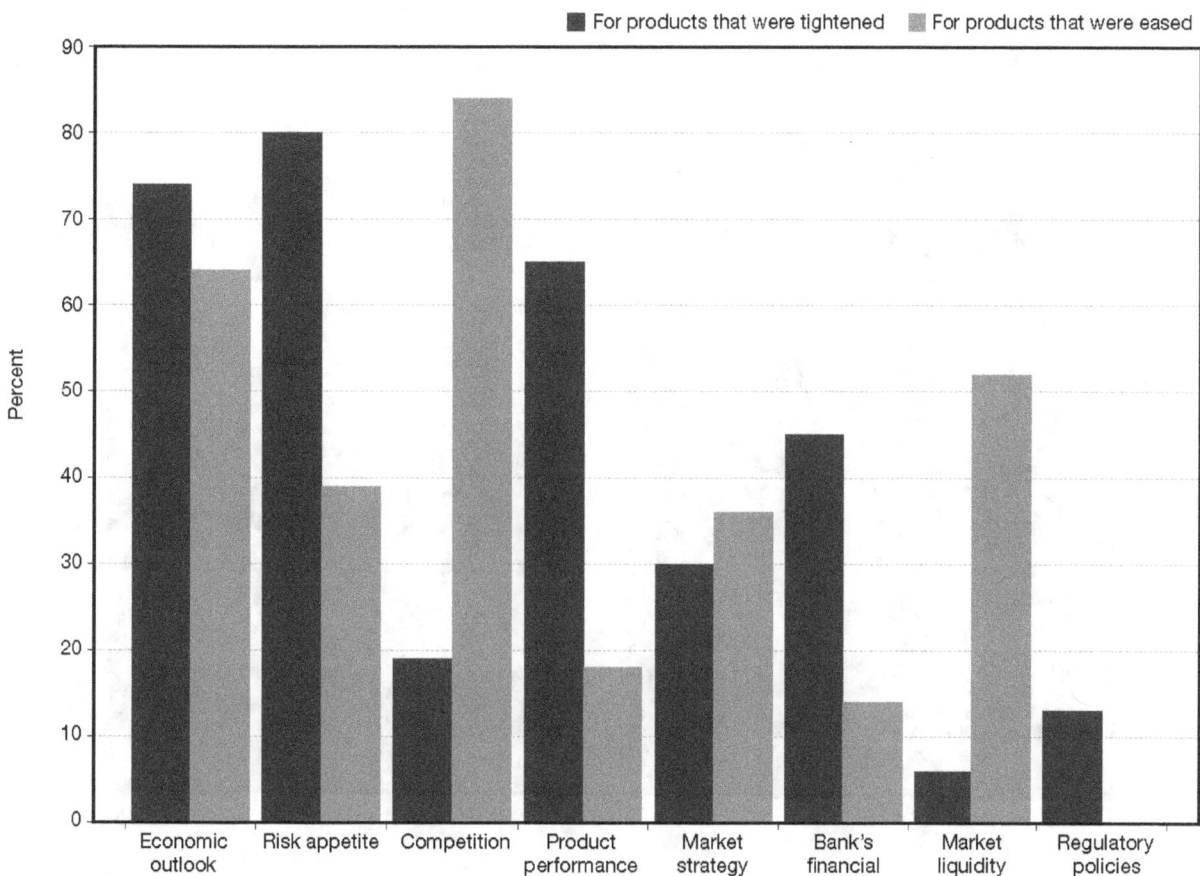

Figure 4: Methods Used to Change Commercial Underwriting Standards (Percentage of Responses)

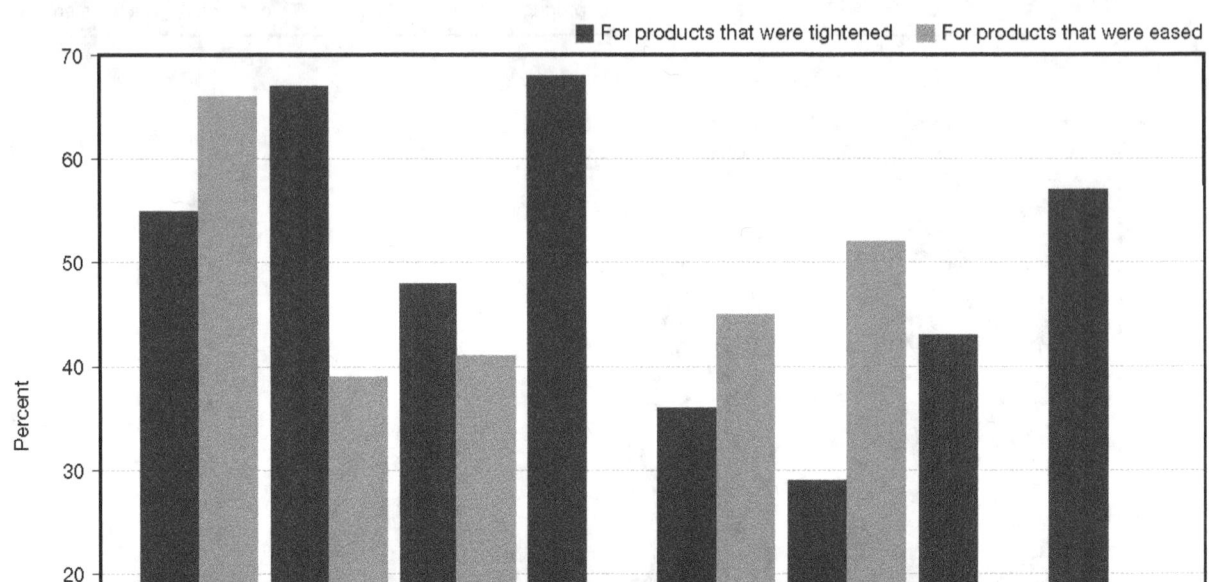

Figure 5: Commercial Credit Risk—Direction of Change and Outlook (Percentage of Responses)

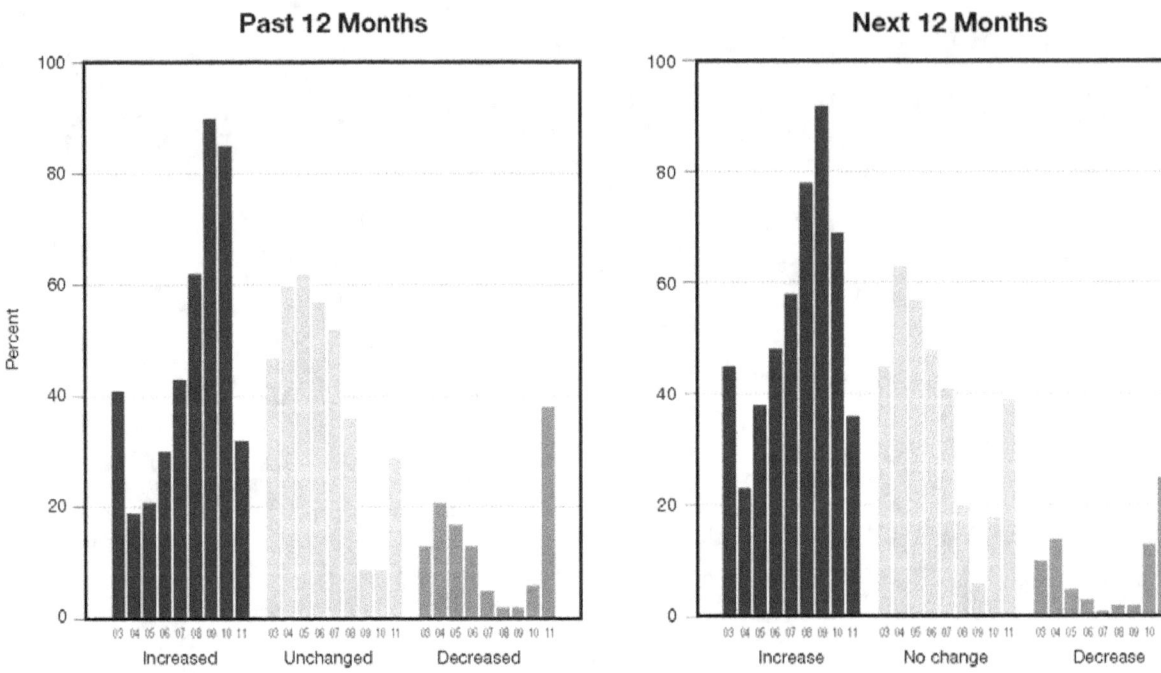

Figure 6: Commercial Credit Risk Trends—Current Credit Risk Change, by Product Type (Percentage of Responses)

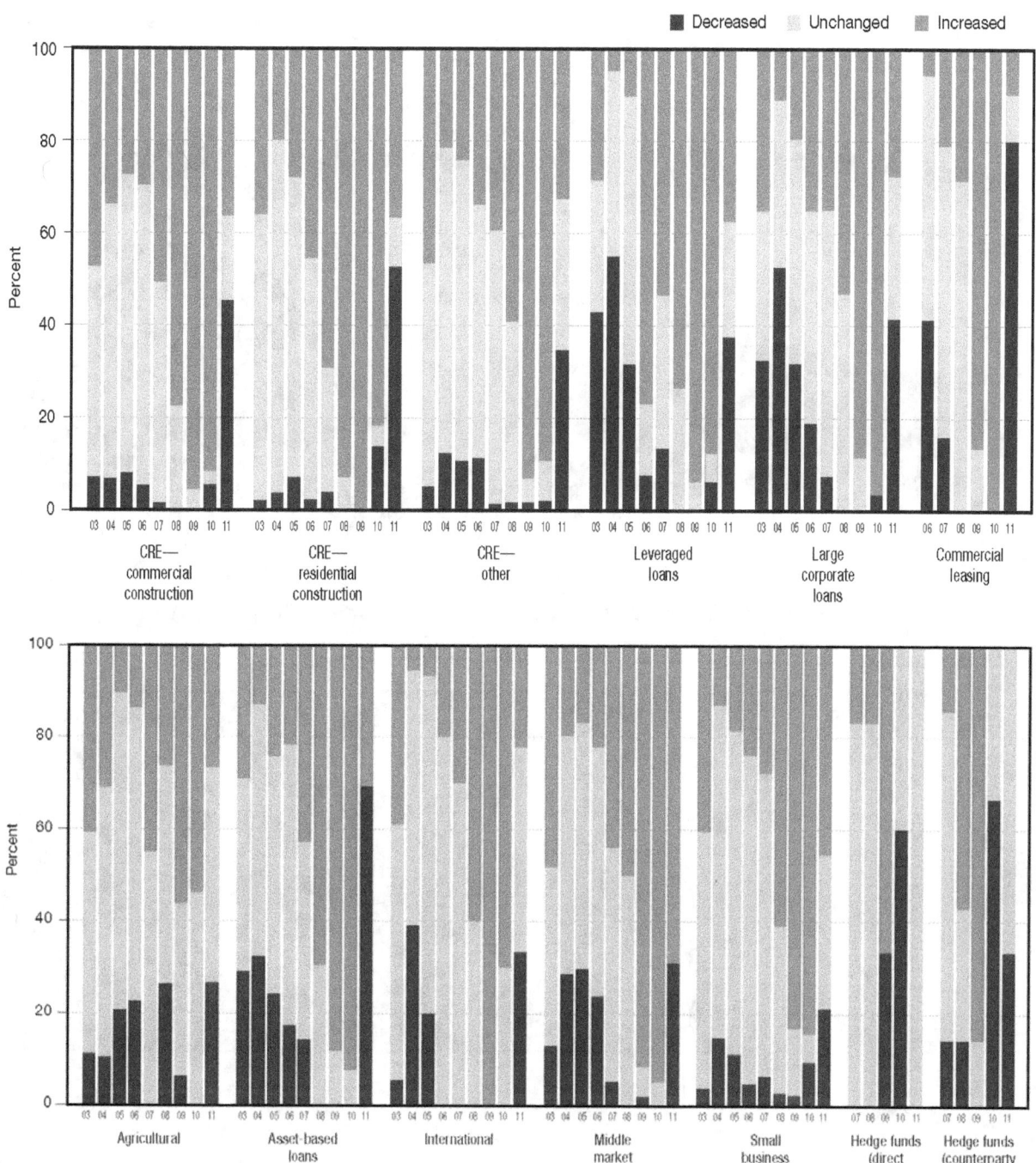

Figure 7: Overall Credit Underwriting Trends—Retail (Percentage of Responses)

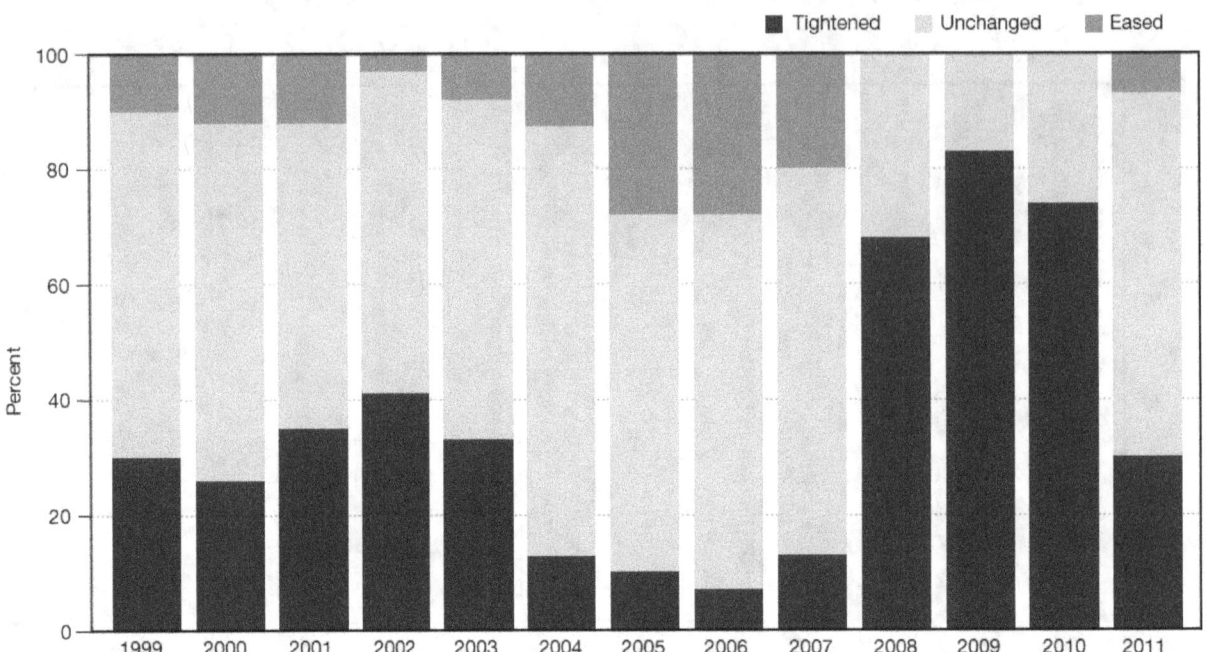

Figure 8: Retail Underwriting Trends, by Product Type (Percentage of Responses)

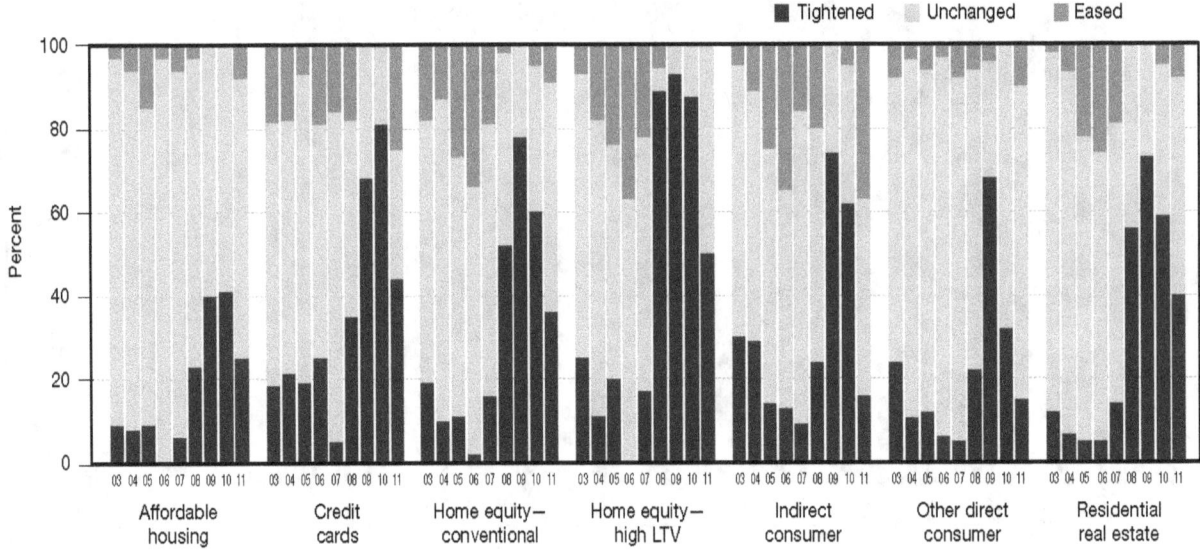

Figure 9: Reasons for Changing Retail Underwriting Standards (Percentage of Responses)

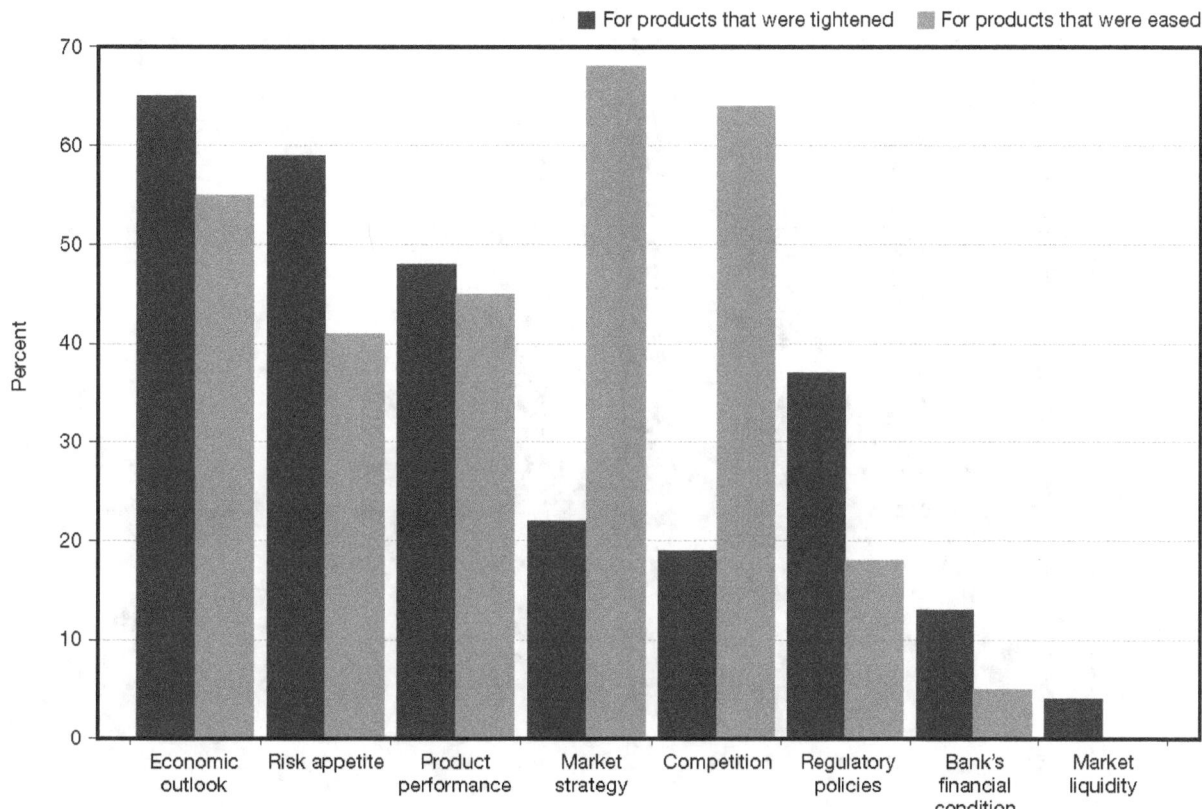

Figure 10: Methods Used to Change Retail Underwriting Standards (Percentage of Responses)

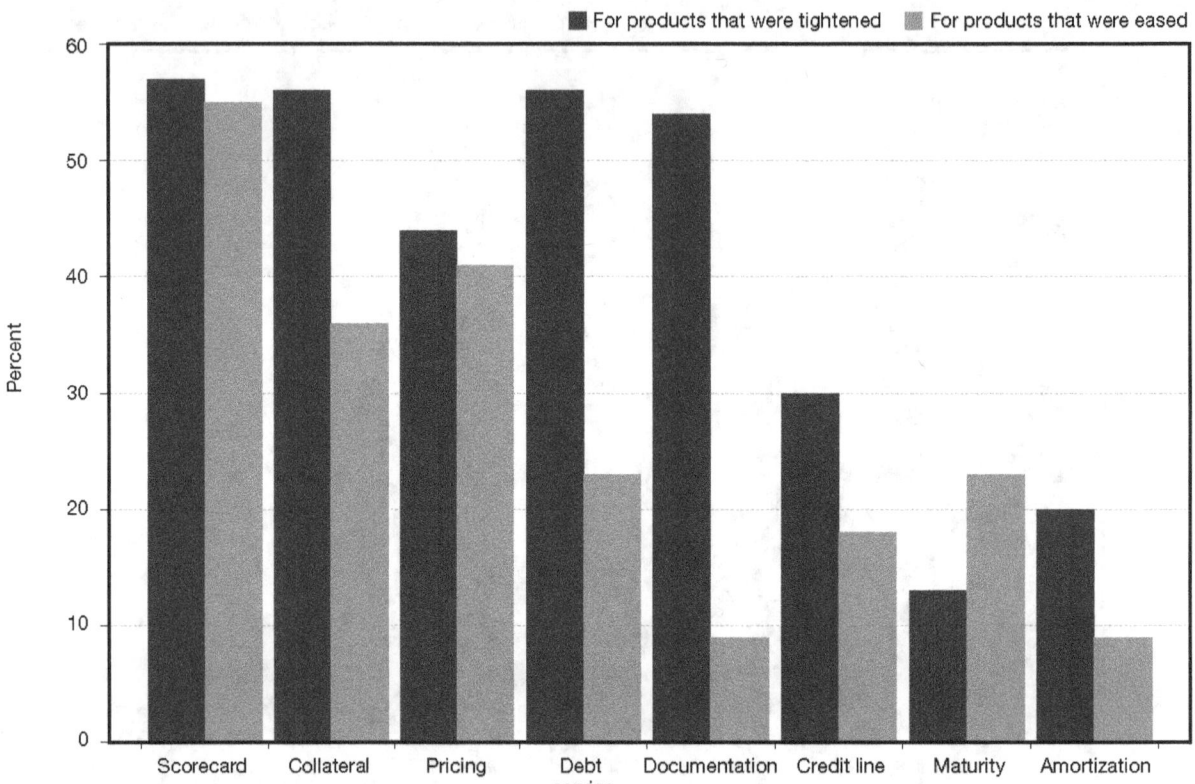

Figure 11: Retail Credit Risk—Direction of Change and Outlook (Percentage of Responses)

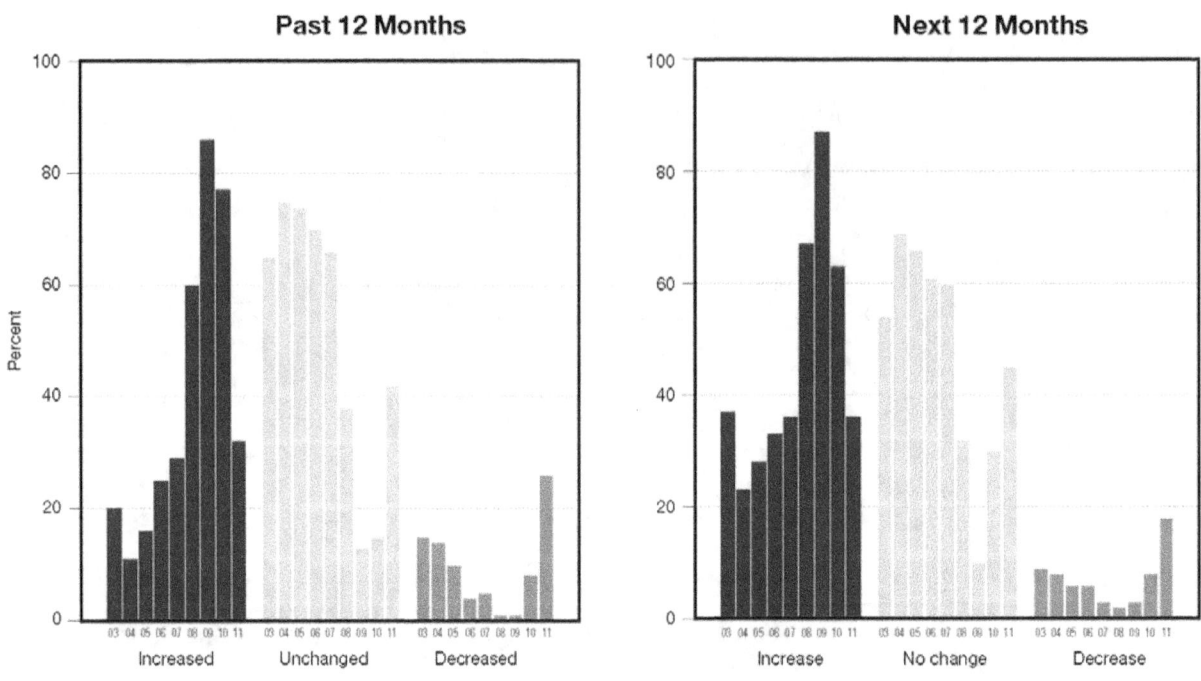

Figure 12: Retail Credit Risk Trends—Current Credit Risk Change, by Product Type (Percentage of Responses)

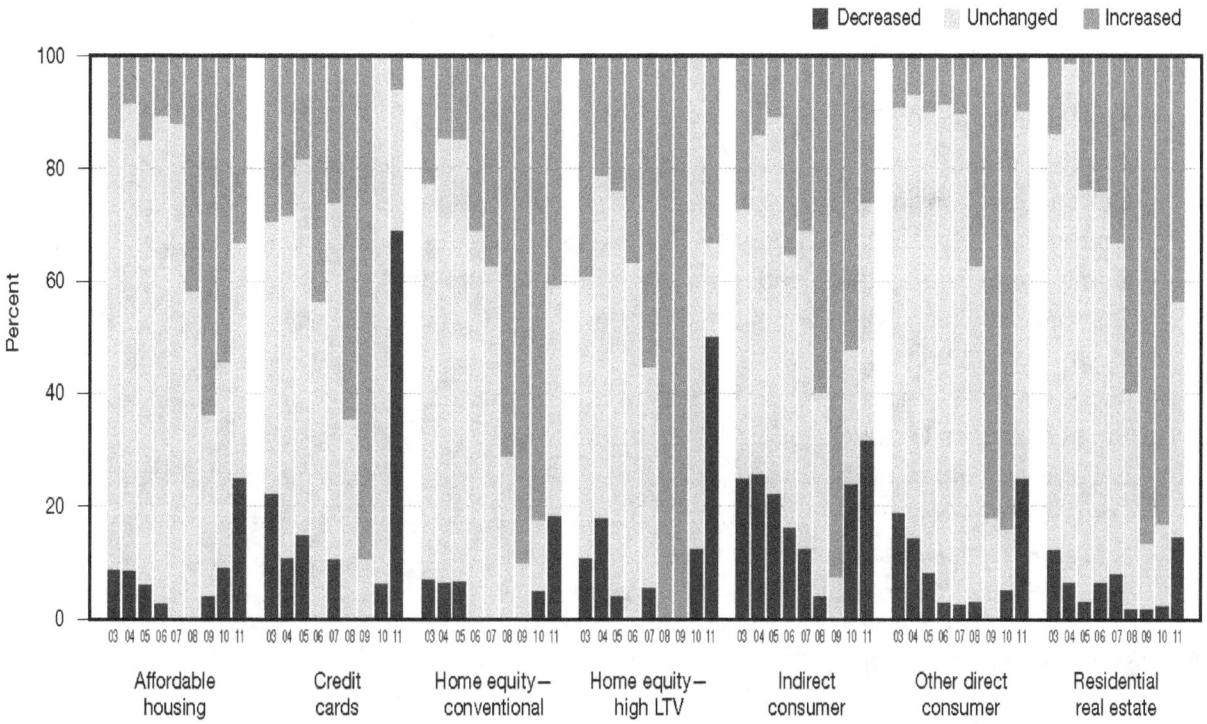

Part III: Data Tables

A. Commercial Lending Portfolios

B. Retail Lending Portfolios

Note: Some percentages in tables and figures do not add to 100 because of rounding.

A. Commercial Lending Portfolios

Agricultural Lending

Fifteen of the 54 surveyed banks met the threshold[1] for reporting on agricultural lending.

Table 13: Changes in Underwriting Standards in Agricultural Loan Portfolios (Percentage of Responses)

	Eased	Unchanged	Tightened
2002	0	70	30
2003	0	67	33
2004	0	93	7
2005	0	93	7
2006	5	95	0
2007	10	80	10
2008	0	95	5
2009	0	75	25
2010	0	54	46
2011	0	80	20

Table 14: Changes in the Level of Credit Risk in Agricultural Loan Portfolios (Percentage of Responses)

	Declined significantly	Declined somewhat	Unchanged	Increased somewhat	Increased significantly
2002	0	7	63	30	0
2003	0	11	48	41	0
2004	0	10	59	31	0
2005	4	17	69	10	0
2006	0	23	63	14	0
2007	0	0	55	45	0
2008	0	26	47	26	0
2009	0	6	38	56	0
2010	0	0	46	31	23
2011	0	27	46	27	0
Future 12 months	0	7	46	47	0

---

[1] Examiners report on loan products greater than 2 percent of the company's committed loan portfolio or more than $10 billion in committed exposure.

Asset-Based Loans

Thirteen surveyed banks met the threshold for reporting on asset-based lending.

**Table 15: Changes in Underwriting Standards in Asset-Based Loan Portfolios
(Percentage of Responses)**

	Eased	Unchanged	Tightened
2002	3	66	31
2003	0	58	42
2004	16	71	13
2005	30	67	3
2006	30	57	13
2007	25	68	7
2008	9	70	22
2009	6	23	71
2010	8	31	61
2011	23	54	23

**Table 16: Changes in the Level of Credit Risk in Asset-Based Loan Portfolios
(Percentage of Responses)**

	Declined significantly	Declined somewhat	Unchanged	Increased somewhat	Increased significantly
2002	0	0	50	50	0
2003	3	26	42	29	0
2004	3	29	55	13	0
2005	0	24	52	24	0
2006	0	17	61	22	0
2007	0	14	43	43	0
2008	0	0	30	70	0
2009	0	0	12	70	18
2010	0	0	8	77	15
2011	0	69	23	8	0
Future 12 months	0	23	62	15	0

Commercial Leasing

Ten of the surveyed banks met the threshold for reporting on commercial leasing.

Table 17: Changes in Underwriting Standards in Commercial Leasing Portfolios (Percentage of Responses)

	Eased	Unchanged	Tightened
2006	12	76	12
2007	26	69	5
2008	7	50	43
2009	0	40	60
2010	0	27	73
2011	10	60	30

Table 18: Changes in the Level of Credit Risk in Commercial Leasing Portfolios (Percentage of Responses)

	Declined significantly	Declined somewhat	Unchanged	Increased somewhat	Increased significantly
2006	6	35	53	6	0
2007	0	16	63	21	0
2008	0	0	71	29	0
2009	0	0	13	80	7
2010	0	0	0	55	45
2011	0	80	10	10	0
Future 12 months	0	50	40	10	0

Commercial Real Estate Lending—Commercial Construction

Thirty-three of the surveyed banks met the threshold for reporting on commercial construction lending.

Table 19: Changes in Underwriting Standards in Commercial Construction Loan Portfolios (Percentage of Responses)

	Eased	Unchanged	Tightened
2003	2	61	37
2004	10	75	15
2005	29	63	8
2006	32	56	12
2007	28	59	13
2008	8	43	49
2009	0	20	80
2010	3	25	72
2011	3	61	36

Table 20: Changes in the Level of Credit Risk in Commercial Construction Loan Portfolios (Percentage of Responses)

	Declined significantly	Declined somewhat	Unchanged	Increased somewhat	Increased significantly
2003	0	7	46	42	5
2004	0	7	59	34	0
2005	2	5	65	28	0
2006	0	5	65	30	0
2007	0	2	48	49	1
2008	0	0	22	69	8
2009	0	0	5	54	41
2010	0	5	3	50	42
2011	6	40	18	33	3
Future 12 months	3	43	24	30	0

Commercial Real Estate Lending—Residential Construction

Nineteen of the surveyed banks met the threshold for reporting on residential construction lending.

Table 21: Changes in Underwriting Standards in Residential Construction Loan Portfolios (Percentage of Responses)

	Eased	Unchanged	Tightened
2003	0	76	24
2004	5	86	9
2005	21	72	7
2006	25	64	11
2007	17	50	33
2008	2	36	62
2009	0	8	92
2010	0	36	64
2011	0	63	37

Table 22: Changes in the Level of Credit Risk in Residential Construction Loan Portfolios (Percentage of Responses)

	Declined significantly	Declined somewhat	Unchanged	Increased somewhat	Increased significantly
2003	0	2	62	34	2
2004	0	4	76	18	2
2005	2	6	65	27	0
2006	0	2	52	46	0
2007	0	4	27	63	6
2008	0	0	7	48	45
2009	0	0	0	34	66
2010	5	9	4	41	41
2011	5	47	11	32	5
Future 12 months	0	42	37	21	0

Commercial Real Estate Lending—Other

Fifty-two of the surveyed banks met the threshold for reporting on other commercial real estate lending.

Table 23: Changes in Underwriting Standards in Other Commercial Real Estate Loan Portfolios (Percentage of Responses)

	Eased	Unchanged	Tightened
2003	5	71	24
2004	8	83	9
2005	24	65	11
2006	32	60	8
2007	20	73	7
2008	2	73	25
2009	2	22	76
2010	2	38	60
2011	9	58	33

Table 24: Changes in the Level of Credit Risk in Other Commercial Real Estate Loan Portfolios (Percentage of Responses)

	Declined significantly	Declined somewhat	Unchanged	Increased somewhat	Increased significantly
2003	0	5	48	43	4
2004	0	12	66	20	2
2005	2	9	65	24	0
2006	1	10	55	34	0
2007	0	2	59	38	1
2008	0	2	39	58	2
2009	0	2	5	67	26
2010	0	2	9	55	34
2011	2	33	33	23	9
Future 12 months	0	29	38	33	0

International Lending

Nine of the surveyed banks met the threshold for reporting on international lending.

Table 25: Changes in Underwriting Standards in International Loan Portfolios (Percentage of Responses)

	Eased	Unchanged	Tightened
2002	11	61	28
2003	6	55	39
2004	11	61	28
2005	27	73	0
2006	30	70	0
2007	30	70	0
2008	10	60	30
2009	0	13	87
2010	30	40	30
2011	56	33	11

Table 26: Changes in the Level of Credit Risk in International Loan Portfolios (Percentage of Responses)

	Declined significantly	Declined somewhat	Unchanged	Increased somewhat	Increased significantly
2002	0	22	39	28	11
2003	0	6	55	33	6
2004	6	33	55	6	0
2005	0	20	73	7	0
2006	0	0	80	20	0
2007	0	0	70	30	0
2008	0	0	40	40	20
2009	0	0	0	63	37
2010	0	0	30	50	20
2011	0	33	45	22	0
Future 12 months	0	0	11	89	0

Middle Market Lending

Forty-two of the surveyed banks met the threshold for reporting on middle market lending.

Table 27: Changes in Underwriting Standards in Middle Market Loan Portfolios (Percentage of Responses)

	Eased	Unchanged	Tightened
2002	0	60	40
2003	6	63	31
2004	14	81	5
2005	28	67	5
2006	31	66	3
2007	33	60	7
2008	6	69	25
2009	0	33	67
2010	0	50	50
2011	19	64	17

Table 28: Changes in the Level of Credit Risk in Middle Market Loan Portfolios (Percentage of Responses)

	Declined significantly	Declined somewhat	Unchanged	Increased somewhat	Increased significantly
2002	2	8	22	66	2
2003	0	13	39	44	4
2004	0	28	52	18	2
2005	4	26	54	16	0
2006	0	24	54	20	2
2007	0	5	51	44	0
2008	0	0	50	48	2
2009	0	2	6	88	4
2010	0	0	5	73	22
2011	0	31	29	38	2
Future 12 months	2	24	41	33	0

Small Business Lending

Thirty-three of the surveyed banks met the threshold for reporting loans in the small business market.

Table 29: Changes in Underwriting Standards in Small Business Loan Portfolios (Percentage of Responses)

	Eased	Unchanged	Tightened
2002	2	66	32
2003	4	65	31
2004	11	74	15
2005	13	81	6
2006	19	76	5
2007	11	76	13
2008	11	72	17
2009	0	36	64
2010	0	34	66
2011	12	55	33

Table 30: Changes in the Level of Credit Risk in Small Business Loan Portfolios (Percentage of Responses)

	Declined significantly	Declined somewhat	Unchanged	Increased somewhat	Increased significantly
2002	0	2	56	40	2
2003	0	4	56	38	2
2004	0	15	72	13	0
2005	0	11	70	19	0
2006	0	5	71	22	2
2007	2	4	66	26	2
2008	0	3	36	58	3
2009	0	2	14	72	12
2010	0	9	6	66	19
2011	0	21	33	46	0
Future 12 months	0	9	55	36	0

Leveraged Loans

Sixteen of the surveyed banks met the threshold for reporting on leveraged loans.

**Table 31: Changes in Underwriting Standards in Leveraged Loan Portfolios
(Percentage of Responses)**

	Eased	Unchanged	Tightened
2002	0	44	56
2003	0	48	52
2004	15	85	0
2005	32	68	0
2006	61	31	8
2007	67	33	0
2008	20	20	60
2009	0	31	69
2010	0	25	75
2011	37	44	19

**Table 32: Changes in the Level of Credit Risk in Leveraged Loan Portfolios
(Percentage of Responses)**

	Declined significantly	Declined somewhat	Unchanged	Increased somewhat	Increased significantly
2002	0	7	26	52	15
2003	10	33	28	29	0
2004	15	40	40	5	0
2005	5	27	58	5	5
2006	0	8	15	69	8
2007	0	13	34	53	0
2008	0	0	27	53	20
2009	0	0	6	63	31
2010	0	6	6	63	25
2011	0	38	25	31	6
Future 12 months	0	6	25	69	0

Large Corporate Loans

Twenty-nine of the surveyed banks met the threshold for reporting the large corporate loans.

Table 33: Changes in Underwriting Standards in Large Corporate Loan Portfolios (Percentage of Responses)

	Eased	Unchanged	Tightened
2002	0	45	55
2003	3	49	48
2004	17	66	17
2005	32	68	0
2006	49	51	0
2007	40	60	0
2008	6	62	32
2009	0	40	60
2010	3	38	59
2011	38	55	7

Table 34: Changes in the Level of Credit Risk in Large Corporate Loan Portfolios (Percentage of Responses)

	Declined significantly	Declined somewhat	Unchanged	Increased somewhat	Increased significantly
2002	0	8	29	53	10
2003	5	27	33	30	5
2004	17	36	36	11	0
2005	5	27	49	19	0
2006	0	19	46	32	3
2007	0	8	57	35	0
2008	0	0	47	47	6
2009	0	0	12	77	11
2010	0	3	0	76	21
2011	0	41	31	28	0
Future 12 months	0	24	38	38	0

Hedge Funds (Direct Credit Exposure)

Three of the surveyed banks met the threshold for reporting on direct lending to hedge funds.

Table 35: Changes in Underwriting Standards in Hedge Funds (Direct Credit Exposure) (Percentage of Responses)

	Eased	Unchanged	Tightened
2007	17	66	17
2008	0	100	0
2009	0	17	83
2010	0	40	60
2011	0	100	0

Table 36: Changes in the Level of Credit Risk in Hedge Funds (Direct Credit Exposure) (Percentage of Responses)

	Declined significantly	Declined somewhat	Unchanged	Increased somewhat	Increased significantly
2007	0	0	83	17	0
2008	0	0	83	17	0
2009	33	0	0	34	33
2010	20	40	40	0	0
2011	0	0	100	0	0
Future 12 months	0	0	67	33	0

Hedge Funds (Counterparty Credit Exposure)

Three of the surveyed banks met the threshold for reporting on counterparty credit exposures to hedge funds.

Table 37: Changes in Underwriting Standards in Hedge Funds (Counterparty Credit Exposure) (Percentage of Responses)

	Eased	Unchanged	Tightened
2007	29	71	0
2008	0	29	71
2009	0	14	86
2010	33	50	17
2011	0	100	0

Table 38: Changes in the Level of Credit Risk in Hedge Funds (Counterparty Credit Exposure) (Percentage of Responses)

	Declined significantly	Declined somewhat	Unchanged	Increased somewhat	Increased significantly
2007	0	14	72	14	0
2008	0	14	29	43	14
2009	0	0	14	57	29
2010	17	50	33	0	0
2011	0	33	67	0	0
Future 12 months	0	0	33	67	0

B. Retail Lending Portfolios

Affordable Housing Lending

Twelve of the surveyed banks met the threshold for reporting on affordable housing lending.

Table 39: Changes in Underwriting Standards in Affordable Housing Loan Portfolios (Percentage of Responses)

	Eased	Unchanged	Tightened
2002	3	91	6
2003	3	88	9
2004	6	86	8
2005	15	76	9
2006	3	97	0
2007	6	88	6
2008	3	74	23
2009	0	60	40
2010	0	59	41
2011	8	67	25

Table 40: Changes in the Level of Credit Risk in Affordable Housing Loan Portfolios (Percentage of Responses)

	Declined significantly	Declined somewhat	Unchanged	Increased somewhat	Increased significantly
2002	0	6	73	21	0
2003	0	9	76	15	0
2004	0	9	82	9	0
2005	0	6	79	15	0
2006	0	3	86	11	0
2007	0	0	88	12	0
2008	0	0	58	35	6
2009	0	4	32	52	12
2010	0	9	36	46	9
2011	0	25	42	33	0
Future 12 months	0	17	58	25	0

Credit Card Lending

Sixteen of the surveyed banks met the threshold for reporting on credit card lending.

Table 41: Changes in Underwriting Standards in Credit Card Loan Portfolios (Percentage of Responses)

	Eased	Unchanged	Tightened
2002	12	66	22
2003	19	62	19
2004	18	61	21
2005	7	74	19
2006	19	56	25
2007	16	79	5
2008	18	47	35
2009	0	32	68
2010	0	19	81
2011	25	31	44

Table 42: Changes in the Level of Credit Risk in Credit Card Loan Portfolios (Percentage of Responses)

	Declined significantly	Declined somewhat	Unchanged	Increased somewhat	Increased significantly
2002	0	6	54	31	9
2003	0	22	48	30	0
2004	0	11	61	25	3
2005	0	15	67	18	0
2006	0	0	56	44	0
2007	0	11	63	26	0
2008	0	0	35	65	0
2009	0	0	10	53	37
2010	0	6	0	63	31
2011	0	69	25	0	6
Future 12 months	6	19	56	19	0

Other Direct Consumer Lending

Twenty of the surveyed banks met the threshold for reporting on other direct consumer lending.

Table 43: Changes in Underwriting Standards in Other Direct Consumer Loan Portfolios (Percentage of Responses)

	Eased	Unchanged	Tightened
2002	2	67	31
2003	8	68	24
2004	3	86	11
2005	6	82	12
2006	3	91	6
2007	8	87	5
2008	6	72	22
2009	4	28	68
2010	0	68	32
2011	10	75	15

Table 44: Changes in the Level of Credit Risk in Other Direct Consumer Loan Portfolios (Percentage of Responses)

	Declined significantly	Declined somewhat	Unchanged	Increased somewhat	Increased significantly
2002	2	6	67	25	0
2003	2	17	72	7	2
2004	2	13	78	7	0
2005	0	8	82	10	0
2006	0	3	88	9	0
2007	0	3	87	10	0
2008	0	3	59	38	0
2009	0	0	18	68	14
2010	0	5	11	74	10
2011	0	25	65	10	0
Future 12 months	0	10	75	15	0

Home Equity—Conventional Lending

Forty-four of the surveyed banks met the threshold for reporting on the conventional home equity lending product.

Table 45: Changes in Underwriting Standards in Home Equity—Conventional Loan Portfolios (Percentage of Responses)

	Eased	Unchanged	Tightened
2002	0	74	26
2003	18	63	19
2004	13	77	10
2005	27	62	11
2006	34	64	2
2007	19	65	16
2008	2	46	52
2009	0	22	78
2010	5	35	60
2011	9	55	36

Table 46: Changes in the Level of Credit Risk in Home Equity—Conventional Loan Portfolios (Percentage of Responses)

	Declined significantly	Declined somewhat	Unchanged	Increased somewhat	Increased significantly
2002	0	7	71	22	0
2003	4	4	69	23	0
2004	0	6	79	13	2
2005	0	7	78	15	0
2006	0	0	69	29	2
2007	0	0	63	34	3
2008	0	0	29	52	19
2009	0	0	10	63	27
2010	0	5	12	73	10
2011	0	18	41	41	0
Future 12 months	0	18	43	39	0

Home Equity—High LTV Lending

Six of the surveyed banks met the threshold for reporting on the high LTV home equity lending product.

Table 47: Changes in Underwriting Standards in Home Equity—High LTV Loan Portfolios (Percentage of Responses)

	Eased	Unchanged	Tightened
2002	0	56	44
2003	7	68	25
2004	18	71	11
2005	24	56	20
2006	37	63	0
2007	22	61	17
2008	6	6	89
2009	0	7	93
2010	0	13	87
2011	0	50	50

Table 48: Changes in the Level of Credit Risk in Home Equity—High LTV Loan Portfolios (Percentage of Responses)

	Declined significantly	Declined somewhat	Unchanged	Increased somewhat	Increased significantly
2002	0	12	40	44	4
2003	0	11	50	36	3
2004	0	18	61	18	3
2005	0	4	72	24	0
2006	0	0	63	37	0
2007	0	6	39	55	0
2008	0	0	0	56	44
2009	0	0	0	36	64
2010	0	13	0	50	37
2011	17	33	17	33	0
Future 12 months	0	66	17	17	0

Indirect Consumer Lending

Nineteen of the surveyed banks met the threshold for reporting on indirect consumer lending.

Table 49: Changes in Underwriting Standards in Indirect Consumer Loan Portfolios (Percentage of Responses)

	Eased	Unchanged	Tightened
2002	0	72	28
2003	5	65	30
2004	11	60	29
2005	25	61	14
2006	35	52	13
2007	16	75	9
2008	20	56	24
2009	0	26	74
2010	5	33	62
2011	37	47	16

Table 50: Changes in the Level of Credit Risk in Indirect Consumer Loan Portfolios (Percentage of Responses)

	Declined significantly	Declined somewhat	Unchanged	Increased somewhat	Increased significantly
2002	3	13	38	43	3
2003	5	20	47	28	0
2004	0	26	60	14	0
2005	3	19	67	8	3
2006	6	10	48	36	0
2007	0	3	87	10	0
2008	0	4	36	60	0
2009	0	0	7	74	19
2010	0	24	24	47	5
2011	0	32	42	26	0
Future 12 months	0	16	32	47	5

Residential Real Estate Lending

Forty-eight of the surveyed banks met the threshold for reporting on residential real estate lending.

Table 51: Changes in Underwriting Standards in Residential Real Estate Loan Portfolios (Percentage of Responses)

	Eased	Unchanged	Tightened
2002	4	83	13
2003	2	86	12
2004	7	86	7
2005	22	73	5
2006	26	69	5
2007	19	67	14
2008	0	44	56
2009	0	27	73
2010	5	36	59
2011	8	52	40

Table 52: Changes in the Level of Credit Risk in Residential Real Estate Loan Portfolios (Percentage of Responses)

	Declined significantly	Declined somewhat	Unchanged	Increased somewhat	Increased significantly
2002	0	8	68	24	0
2003	0	12	74	12	2
2004	0	6	92	2	0
2005	0	3	73	24	0
2006	0	7	69	24	0
2007	2	6	59	33	0
2008	2	0	38	55	5
2009	0	2	12	69	17
2010	0	3	14	57	26
2011	0	15	42	39	4
Future 12 months	0	15	37	48	0

www.ingramcontent.com/pod-product-compliance
Lightning Source LLC
Chambersburg PA
CBHW052017280526
45793CB00005B/1022